FIRST STEPS
OF
Faith

Learning to Walk with Jesus

CANDY WARREN
&
CAROLYN WILEY

ROSE & PEARL

Publishing

Cover design and photo by Carolyn Wiley.

Author photo by Evelyn Wiley.

The Ruby Tent is an imprint of Rose and Pearl Publishing, LLC.

First Steps of Faith: Learning to Walk with Jesus
Copyright © 2023, Rose and Pearl Publishing, LLC
A Bible study in The Ruby Tent
Published by Rose and Pearl Publishing, LLC
Senatobia, Mississippi 38668
www.roseandpearl.net

ISBN 979-8-9894343-0-5 (paperback)
ISBN 979-8-9894343-1-2 (hardcover)
ISBN 979-8-9894343-2-9 (ebook)

Dedication

To John Warren, Bryan Wiley, and Mel Cowan - without the three of you, this book would not have happened

To new believers - may your walk with Jesus grow and thrive more each day

Hello!

We are

CANDY WARREN
&
CAROLYN WILEY

We are a mother and daughter who have navigated numerous trials together while growing in our faith. We've had the privilege of investing in the lives of other women, just as our lives have been enriched by one another and our sisters in Christ. Through this Bible study, we aim to provide encouragement as you embark on your initial steps in your faith journey.

rt

TABLE OF CONTENTS

rt

ABOUT THE RUBY TENT

The Ruby Tent is an online learning community for Christian women. It provides courses and an opportunity to build a community that helps women grow and integrate their faith into their daily lives. The course catalog is growing regularly to include Bible studies and courses on growing in your faith.

The name "The Ruby Tent" comes from ancient Jewish culture's idea of a "Red Tent," In this online tent, we seek to build a place where women grow together under the shelter of the Almighty, connected by the blood of Jesus.

In Proverbs 31:10 (KJV), the author asks, "A virtuous woman, who can find? For her worth is far above rubies." Thus, the ruby tent, a shade of red, symbolizes the priceless worth of women.

Join us at <u>therubytent.com</u>, or find us on Social Media as @therubytent. Scan the QR code to go to our website.

# HOW DO I BECOME SAVED?

What does it mean "to be saved?" Saved from what? "For the wages of sin is death" (Romans 6:23). Thus, if you have sinned, even once, even if you are a 'good person,' then you have to pay for that sin with your death - eternal separation from the Creator, Almighty God. So, have you sinned? The Bible tells us that "all have sinned and fall short of the glory of God" (Romans 3:23). Thus, we are all facing God's eternal wrath, even those of who are 'good people.'

BUT!

"We shall be saved from the wrath of God through Him" (Romans 5:9, KJV). That 'Him' is Jesus! "Because, if you confess with your mouth that Jesus is Lord and believe in your heart that God raised him from the dead, you will be saved" (Romans 10:9). That's what Jesus' sacrifice does. It replaces our sinfulness with Jesus' perfect righteousness, making us righteous before God. Giving us a value above rubies. Here's an acrostic using RUBY to show you should go about being saved:

R - Repent (turn away from your sin)
U - Utter (verbally confess that Jesus is Lord)
B - Believe (trust Jesus' sacrifice redeemed you)
Y - Yield (allow Jesus to take control of your life)

First Steps

Coming to saving faith in Jesus is as simple as accepting a gift from a loved one. Jesus paid for this gift of forgiveness and eternal life with his death on the cross and resurrection. All we have to do is accept this gift.

Where this analogy ends, however, is that knowing Jesus as our Lord and Savior is not just a one-time transaction. It is a relationship. Jesus wants us to walk with him daily, get to know him, and experience him on such an intimate level that it affects everything about our lives.

Have you ever fallen in love or been so obsessed with something that it was all you thought about? When you love something that much, you want to know everything about it. You dream about it. You read about it. You memorize every tidbit of information you can find. That is the type of relationship God wants to have with you. And just like falling in love, it does not happen all at once. The feelings grow as the relationship grows. You sometimes stumble and fall. But just like learning to walk, all it takes is to get back up again.

In this Bible study, we will walk with you as you take those first steps in growing your relationship with God from that just-getting-to-know-you phase to a more intimate daily walk with Jesus.

We will explore four fundamental aspects of your faith journey in this study - prayer, reading scripture, finding a church home, and finding companions on your journey. Each chapter of this study is devoted to one of these aspects, divided into five days of short daily devotionals.

In addition to this book, there is a short course on the First Steps of Faith at www.therubytent.com. The course corresponds to this book and is self-paced, with videos and downloadable resources. Though each can stand alone, you will maximize your study by pairing this workbook with the video lessons and interactive community.

Come join your sisters at

THE RUBY TENT

But Jesus Himself would often slip away to the wilderness and PRAY.

Luke 5:16 (NASB)

Prayer

Prayer is our communication with the Living God. How many people of high importance do you get to talk to whenever you feel like it? Even the daughter of an earthly king or president wouldn't be able to run to her father's arms while he is in the middle of a meeting. But as daughters of the King of Kings, we can! Prayer gives us access to Him at any moment of the day, even if He currently is talking to another world leader.

In this chapter, we will learn:

☑ What prayer is and why we should pray,

☑ How Jesus taught us to pray,

☑ To pray for God's will, guidance, and provision,

☑ An acronym to remember how to pray, and

☑ A simple method to remember who to pray for.

Father, thank you that we can run to you whenever we want. That you not only allow us this chance to talk to you, but you are eager to hear from us! Amen.

Day 1

TEACH - *Let's learn*

What is prayer, and why is it important? Do you know of any healthy relationships that do not involve communication? Can you imagine a world without communication? It is the connection in every relationship. We talk on our phones, on social media, through texts and direct messages. We speak to babies while they are still in the womb. Surely, we should be talking to the Creator.

Prayer is simply that—talking to God. It is an essential element to having a relationship with Him. He has communicated with us since Adam! He spoke the world into existence. He guided Adam and those who came after Adam by speaking to them. He spoke to the prophets and had many men record His words so that we could know Him. But He doesn't want a one-way conversation. He wants us to talk to Him as well!

> "...casting all your care upon Him, for He careth for you."
> 1 Peter 5:7, KJV

So, what do we say when talking to the One who is all-knowing and all-powerful? We can tell Him anything! He already knows, after

all, so there is no need to try to hide our thoughts and feelings from Him. We can ask for whatever we need or want. "Ask, and it will be given to you; seek, and you will find; knock, and it will be opened to you. For everyone who asks receives, and the one who seeks finds, and to the one who knocks it will be opened. Or which one of you, if his son asks him for bread, will give him a stone? Or if he asks for a fish, will give him a serpent? If you then, who are evil, know how to give good gifts to your children, how much more will your Father who is in heaven give good things to those who ask him" (Matthew 7:1-11). God does not always give us what we ask, however. He gives according to His will.

God's guidance on what He desires us to pray about is laid out in 1 Peter 5:7 (KJV): "...casting all your care upon Him, for He careth for you." So, as you release your concerns, you can find tranquility and the certainty that God will respond. But remember, part of the process involves attentively awaiting His response.

KEY POINTS
- Prayer is talking to God.
- Jesus prayed.
- He tells us to cast our cares on Him.

The main reason we should pray is simple - Jesus did. If the God of all creation dedicated time to pray during His time on earth, seeking to align with the Father's will, then it's a practice we should embrace, too. As written, "But Jesus Himself would often slip away to the wilderness and pray" (Luke 5:16, NASB).

Another straightforward reason to pray is that He instructs us to do so! As scripture says, "Do not be anxious about anything, but in everything by prayer and supplication with thanksgiving let your requests be made known to God" (Philippians 4:6).

Bowing your head, closing your eyes, kneeling, or standing - these postures aren't essential for getting through to God. Your prayer might flow like a melodious song, burst like a triumphant shout, or whisper like a gentle breeze. Regardless of your approach, the key thing is simply that we pray.

ENRICH - *Let's learn more*

Look up the following verses. What do they tell you about prayer? Write out what you learn on the lines below. Matthew 26:41; 1 Thessalonians 5:16-18; 1 John 5:14; Jeremiah 33:3

NURTURE - *Let's apply it to our lives*

You might have already noticed that a brief prayer is provided for you at the beginning of each chapter in this devotional. Also, at the end of each lesson, you'll find a space to write a concise prayer centered around your daily insights. This practice of praying about what you've learned is intended to safeguard against our enemy, Satan, who seeks to steal and destroy the growth we've attained.

Let's put this into action. Here's an example of a prayer for today's lesson. Use it as a guide to compose your prayer below: "Dear Lord, I am grateful for the gift of prayer and for Your desire not only to listen to us but to speak to us. Please engrain within me a constant recollection of all I'm gaining from these lessons. Amen."

THANKS - *Let's thank God for this wisdom*

In the box below, write a short prayer thanking God for what He has revealed to you today and asking Him for further insight.

Day 2

TEACH - *Let's learn*

What are we to pray for? Jesus gave us a model prayer in Matthew 6:9-13 (KJV). In this prayer, Jesus taught us what to pray for. Let's look at the 'whats' below.

> Our Father which art in heaven,
> Hallowed be thy name.
> Thy kingdom come.
> Thy will be done in earth,
> as it is in heaven.
> Give us this day our daily bread.
> And forgive us our debts,
> as we forgive our debtors.
> And lead us not into temptation,
> but deliver us from evil:
> For thine is the kingdom, and the power,
> and the glory, for ever. Amen.

God's Will
God's Forgiveness
God's Guidance
God's Provision
God's Deliverance

In these verses, Jesus prayed for five things:
- God's will,
- God's provision,
- God's forgiveness,
- God's guidance, and
- God's deliverance.

Today and tomorrow, we will look briefly at these five things and learn how to pray for each one as Jesus did.

God's Will

What is the will of God? Does that seem so big and complex that it is unknowable to us mere mortals? The good news is that God tells us what His will is for us, and it is neither unknowable nor complex.

"For this is the will of my Father, that everyone who looks on the Son and believes in him should have eternal life, and I will raise him up on the last day" (John 6.40). That's great news! Additionally, He tells us, "For this is the will of God, your sanctification..." (1 Thessalonians 4:3). Sanctification means becoming more like Jesus. It is the work of the Holy Spirit in every believer. Thus, God wants us to have eternal life and become more like His son.

> "For this is the will of my Father, that everyone who looks on the Son and believes in him should have eternal life."
> John 6:40

Lastly, in Micah, God tells us he requires three things of us: "He has told you, O man, what is good; and what does the Lord require of you but to do justice, and to love kindness, and to walk humbly with your God" (Micah 6:8). These three things are characteristics you will have as the Holy Spirit works in your life to make you more like Jesus. This Bible study is about beginning that walk with God.

There are verses in the Bible you can use to help you pray for God's will. Colossians 1:9 reads, "And so, from the day we heard, we have not ceased to pray for you, asking that you may be filled with the knowledge of His will in all spiritual wisdom and understanding." Likewise, Psalm 143:10 states, "Teach me to do your will, For you are my God! Let your good Spirit lead me on level ground!" You can use these two verses as a starting point for your prayers about God's will.

God's Guidance

What is the difference between God's will and God's guidance? Think of God's will as His overall plan. Then, we need His guidance each day as we seek to live a life that is in keeping with his overall plan. Do I accept a job, marry a particular person, or move to a specific city? Though there might be many different options for these choices that are not bad nor sinful, God can and wants to guide you to make choices that are best for you and are in keeping with His overall plan for your eternal life and sanctification.

KEY POINTS
- The Lord's Prayer is our model
- Jesus prayed for God's will, guidance, forgiveness, provision, and deliverance.

"Trust in the LORD with all your heart, and do not lean on your own understanding. In all your ways acknowledge Him, and He will make straight your paths" (Proverbs 3:5-6). "I will instruct you and teach you in the way you should go; I will counsel you with My eye upon you" (Psalm 32:8). Thus, God promises that if we ask Him, He will show us what we need to do throughout our lives. By living in a relationship with Him, we will know His good and perfect will for us each day.

ENRICH - *Let's learn more*

Look up Psalm 25:9. What attitude does God expect of those He guides? Psalm 19:8 tells us two benefits for those who follow God's guidance. What are they? Psalm 119:105 tells us what God uses to guide us. What is it? Summarize your answers below.

NURTURE - *Let's apply it to our lives*

What is the hardest part for you in knowing God's guidance for your life? What have you learned today that can make knowing God's will and His plan for your life easier?

THANKS - *Let's thank God for this wisdom*

In the box below, write a short prayer thanking God for what He has revealed to you today and asking Him for further insight.

Day 3

TEACH - *Let's learn*

Yesterday, we looked at the model prayer Jesus gave us in the Sermon on the Mount. We saw how we can pray for God's will to be done and seek His guidance. Today, we will examine God's forgiveness, deliverance, and provision.

God's Forgiveness

"If we confess our sins, He is faithful and righteous, so that He will forgive us our sins and cleanse us from all unrighteousness" (1 John 1:9). Everyone sins. Everyone. Some people's sins are more public than others, such as adultery scandals. Other sins are more private and may never be known to those around us, such as harboring hatred towards someone you rarely see. Either way, scripture makes it clear that to be forgiven of our sins, we must confess those sins to God. But thank you, Lord, that you promise us forgiveness! Thus, prayer should include asking for forgiveness for the sins we know of and repenting those sins.

At this point, you might think, "Wait a minute - 'sins that we know of'? Does that mean that there are sins we don't know about?" Actually, yes. Before you get too concerned, we are talking about thoughts and actions that you are aware of but might not have realized are sinful. God will reveal what is sinful.

"Let us test and examine our ways, and return to the LORD!" (Lamentations 3:40). In the book of Lamentations, the prophet Jeremiah lamented (hence the name) over the sins of the nation of

Israel. He implored the people to reflect on their lives and seek repentance for anything that deviated from God's Word. We are called to do the same. "Search me, O God, and know my heart! Try me and know my thoughts" (Psalms 139:23). When we pray and beseech God to examine our hearts, He will reveal those aspects of our lives that require repentance. He graciously guides us toward the path of righteousness and calls us to return to Him.

> "Let us test and examine our ways, and return to the LORD!"
> Lam 3:40

God's Deliverance

King David faced numerous adversaries and frequently experienced persecution. In Psalm 69:14 (KJV), he fervently pleads, "Rescue me from the mire; do not let me sink; let me be delivered from those who hate me, and out of these deep waters." Likewise, in Psalm 142:6, he implores, "Attend to my cry, for I am brought very low! Deliver me from my persecutors, for they are too strong for me!" Have you ever found yourself in a situation where you needed God's deliverance? Have you prayed for that deliverance?

Deliverance is an outcome of confession and repentance, but it might not always occur immediately. There could be a purpose behind the situation that God has allowed us to be in. Just as God used David's challenges to impart valuable lessons that shaped him into the remarkable king he became, our trials may serve as opportunities for growth.

Alternatively, we might still be trapped in our predicament even after God has provided a way out. This could be because we're unwilling to use the escape God has placed before us. Perhaps the path to freedom involves leaving a stressful job or ending a romantic relationship that doesn't align with God's plan for us. Carolyn experienced both scenarios, and she can attest that the pain of using God's escape was intense. However, in hindsight, the transformation and growth that resulted from these decisions were undeniably worth it.

KEY POINTS
- Through Jesus, God's forgiveness is always available to those who confess and repent.
- God will deliver us but in His way and in His timing.
- God provides for all our needs.

God's Provision

Provision takes on various forms. In Genesis 27:28, the prayer reads, "May God give you of the dew of heaven and of the fatness of the earth and plenty of grain and wine." Similarly, in Romans 15:13, Paul prays, "May the God of hope fill you with all joy and peace in believing, so that by the power of the Holy Spirit you may abound in hope." Whether it's sustenance, hope, or strength that you require, God is the ultimate provider.

Seeking His provision is a facet of prayer that most people are familiar with. It's often the first thing that comes to mind when thinking about prayer: "God, I need (fill in the blank)." However, as genuine believers, we must tread carefully. We must prioritize seeking God above all else, allowing Him to be our ultimate provider rather than solely seeking His gifts and loving Him only for what He gives us. He is enough. He is the one who sustains us, not the gifts that He gives us.

In summary, in your prayers, seek God's will, His forgiveness, His provision, His guidance, and His deliverance for yourself and those around you.

ENRICH - *Let's learn more*

Using your Bible or an online tool such as biblegateway.com, find another instance of someone praying for God's provision, deliverance, or forgiveness described in the Bible.

NURTURE - *Let's apply it to our lives*

Picking either forgiveness or deliverance, take a few moments to ask God to show you His path for you in that area. Is there any unconfessed sin? Confess it now. Are you seeking deliverance? Ask God for His deliverance and to give you the courage to follow His path.

THANKS - *Let's thank God for this wisdom*

In the box below, write a short prayer thanking God for what He has revealed to you today and asking Him for further insight.

Day 4

TEACH - *Let's learn*

Today, let's talk about *how* we pray. There are two basic ways to pray. We can pray *without* words, and we can pray *with* words.

Praying without words is a state of mind, an attitude, a posture of both the body and the heart. God encourages us to "pray without ceasing" (1 Thess 5:17). Since it's humanly impossible to maintain a constant verbal dialogue, even within our thoughts, with God 24/7, He must be referring to something more profound—an attitude of prayer. This mindset involves continuously being aware of God's presence and sovereignty, even when you're not directly communicating with Him.

> "Then you will call upon me and come and pray to me, and I will hear you."
> Jer 29:12

Praying *with* words is more straightforward. It involves direct communication with God through our thoughts, spoken words, or written expressions. You can choose to pray silently, vocalize your prayers, or jot them down, as we've encouraged you to do after each day's lesson. We highly recommend keeping a prayer journal if you

still need to start. It doesn't need to be elaborate; a simple $1 spiral notebook serves just as well as a $50 leather-bound one. As your prayers are answered, and you witness God's work in your life, recording those moments becomes invaluable. You'll create a chronicle of your journey with Jesus that can provide encouragement and inspiration during times of testing in your faith.

KEY POINTS
- You can pray with words or without words.
- Praying without words is an attitude of prayer.
- You can use many different models to pray with words.
- The Holy Spirit intercedes for you if you don't have the words.

To organize our prayers, we can use the Lord's prayer from Matthew as our guide to prayer, as we have seen in the last three days. Additionally, there is a concise acrostic that can assist us in recalling the essential components of our prayers - the acrostic PRAY, which stands for:

P - **Praise** God.
R - **Repent** of your sins.
A - **Ask** for God's provision.
Y - **Yield** to God's will in our lives.

Notice that this acrostic includes all the components of the Lord's model prayer.

Praise - "Our Father, who art in heaven, hallowed by thy name." "For thine is the kingdom and the glory and the power forever."

Repent - "Forgive us our debts as we forgive our debtors."
Ask - "Give us this day our daily bread." "Lead us not into temptation but deliver us from evil."
Yield - "Thy kingdom come, thy will be done on earth as it is in heaven."

As we have said before, how you pray is not as important as having the right attitude before God, one of humility and worship. There isn't a right or wrong way to pray as long as you seek God.

ENRICH - *Let's learn more*

There are as many ways to pray as there are people who pray. Do a quick internet search for the acrostic PRAY, and you will see many others pop up. Look through them and make a note of any that appeal to you.

NURTURE - *Let's apply it to our lives*

Using the acrostic PRAY, write a short prayer below on what you want God to teach you through this study.

THANKS - *Let's thank God for this wisdom*

In the box below, write a short prayer thanking God for what He has revealed to you today and asking Him for further insight.

Day 5

TEACH - *Let's learn*

Today, let's delve into another method of structuring our prayers, specifically focusing on the "ASK" portion of our prayer.

You might find yourself with numerous prayer requests, more than you can easily manage. This is one of the compelling reasons to maintain a prayer journal. You can keep a simple, ongoing list of bullet points at the beginning of your journal, reserving the back for your detailed written prayers. However, if you are speaking your prayer aloud and want a "handy" way to remind yourself of your list, you can use your hand!

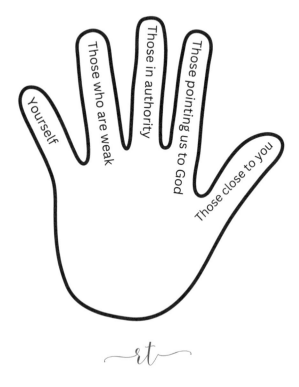

- For your **thumb**, remember "those closest to you." This will remind you to pray for your family and friends.
- For your **pointer finger**, remember "those who point you to God." This will remind you to pray for spiritual leaders like your pastor, missionaries, and other ministers.
- For your **middle finger**, remember "those in authority." This will remind us to pray for those in authority over us in the government or our workplace.
- For your **ring finger**, remember "those who are weak." This will remind us to pray for those who are physically weak (babies, children, the elderly, those who are sick) and the spiritually frail (those who haven't accepted Christ and those who are new in their faith).
- For your **little finger**, remember "yourself."
- Lastly, clench your hand into a **fist**. This powerful gesture serves as a reminder to pray even for our enemies.

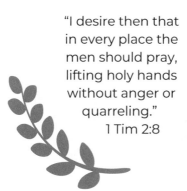

"I desire then that in every place the men should pray, lifting holy hands without anger or quarreling."
1 Tim 2:8

You would use this tool as a memory device, going through each of your fingers and praying for those who come to mind in that category. This tool would be an easy way to teach your children who to pray for, as well.

In this chapter, we learned what prayer is, why we should pray, how to use the Lord's prayer as a model for our prayers, the acrostic PRAY, and a simple memory tool to remind us who to include in our prayers. The next chapter will look at another foundational aspect of growing in our walk with Jesus - reading His Word.

KEY POINTS
- You can use your hand to remember who to pray for.
- How we pray is never as important as our heart before God when we pray.

ENRICH - *Let's learn more*

Want to learn more about prayer? We dive deeper into prayer as your sacrifice, your warfare, your ministry, and your responsibility in our stand-alone study on prayer. This will be part of The Ruby Tent beginning in late 2023. We would love for you to join us!

Come join your sisters at

THE RUBY TENT

NURTURE - *Let's apply it to our lives*

On the drawing of the hand below, write the names of the people in your life associated with each finger.

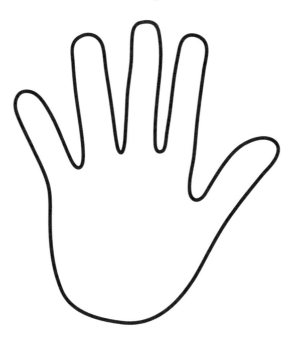

THANKS - *Let's thank God for this wisdom*

In the box below, write a short prayer thanking God for what He has revealed to you today and asking Him for further insight.

In the beginning was *the Word,* and the Word was with God and the Word *was God.*

John 1:1

Reading Scripture

The best way to grow in your relationship with God is by getting to know him better through reading His Word - the Bible. In this week's lesson, we will learn more about the Bible and a simple process for beginning to study God's Word.

In this chapter, we will learn:

- ☑ Why we need to study the Bible,

- ☑ About the parts of the Bible,

- ☑ About the different types of translations,

- ☑ How to get started reading your Bible, and

- ☑ A simple process to take your study deeper.

Father, guide us in learning about your Holy Word through the Holy Spirit. Thank you for giving us your Word to show us your love and to guide and direct us. Amen.

Day 1

TEACH - *Let's learn*

James Merritt put it this way, "The primary purpose of reading the Bible is not to know the Bible but to know God." God gave us the Bible so that we might know Him and, by knowing Him, come to worship and glorify Him alone.

> "All scripture is given by inspiration of God, and is profitable for doctrine, for reproof, for correction, for instruction in righteousness: That the man of God may be perfect, thoroughly furnished unto all good works."
> 2 Timothy 3:16-17 (KJV)

God is the author of the Bible, though He worked through more than 40 different men over a span of 1600 years to transcribe its contents. As 2 Timothy 3:16a (KJV) declares, "All scripture is given by inspiration of God." Therefore, regardless of the human instruments used to document His words, God remains the author of all scripture.

In his second letter to the Thessalonians, the apostle Paul further emphasizes that scripture is unequivocally the Word of God, not the word of man. In 2 Thessalonians 2:13 (KJV), he writes, "For this cause also thank we God without ceasing, because when ye received the Word of God which ye heard of us, ye received it not as the word of men, but as it is in truth, the Word of God, which effectually worketh also in you that believe."

KEY POINTS
- The Bible is inspired by the Holy Spirit.
- It is true, and useful for instruction and correction.

In his book *Strange Fire*, John McArthur explains the process of writing scripture like this: "As those godly men were carried along by the Holy Spirit, He superintended their words and used them to produce the Scriptures. As a sailing ship is carried along by the wind to reach its final destination, so the human authors of Scripture were moved by the Spirit of God to communicate exactly what He desired. In that process, the Spirit filled their minds, souls, and hearts with divine truth— mingling it sovereignly and supernaturally with their unique styles, vocabularies, and experiences, and guiding them to produce a perfect, inerrant result" (*Strange Fire*, 2013, p. 223).

2 Timothy 3:16b-17 (KJV) also outlines the purpose of engaging with the Bible, as it is "profitable for doctrine, for reproof, for correction, for instruction in righteousness: That the man of God may be perfect, thoroughly furnished unto all good works." Billy Graham, the renowned evangelist, underscores the transformative effect of reading the Bible, stating that "the very practice of reading

[the Bible] will have a purifying effect upon your mind and heart. Let nothing take the place of this daily exercise." His statement aligns with the conclusion of 2 Timothy 3:17, where God affirms that the Bible is essential for personal growth and the pursuit of good deeds.

The Bible serves as a refining fire. Just as impurities in silver are burned away in the fire, leaving behind only the pure silver, regular Bible reading and study allow the Holy Spirit to eliminate old sinful patterns and replace them with healthier habits that align with God's character and lead to a more Christ-like life.

ENRICH - *Let's learn more*

Using a Bible app or online Bible resource (such as blueletterbible.org), search for other verses in the Bible that speak to it being written and inspired by God. Note the references on the lines below.

NURTURE - *Let's apply it to our lives*

Do you believe the Bible is the inspired Word of God? When did you come to this belief, or what keeps you from believing this?

THANKS - *Let's thank God for this wisdom*

In the box below, write a short prayer thanking God for what He has revealed to you today and asking Him for further insight.

Day 2

TEACH:

The word "Bible" comes from the Greek word "biblia," which means little books, as the Bible is a collection of 66 smaller books. There are books of law, history, poetry, romance, stories about Jesus, letters to churches and specific people, and books of prophecy telling of future events. The books that are included in the Bible are part of what we refer to as the Canon. This comes from the Greek word "Kanon," which means measuring rod. Therefore, the books that we have in the Bible have been verified by a measuring rod that they are consistent with the teachings of Jesus and accepted by the apostles.

> "...when ye received the Word of God which ye heard of us, ye received it not as the word of men, but as it is in truth, the Word of God..."
> 1 Thess 2:13 (KJV)

The 66 books of the Bible are divided into the Old and New Testaments, or covenants. There is the Old Covenant, given to Abraham, and the New Covenant, fulfilled for us by Jesus. Though the whole Bible points to the life and work of Jesus, the New Testament records his physical life on earth and the activity of the early church after his ascension to heaven. Of the 66 books in the Bible, 39 are in the Old Testament, and 27 are in the New Testament.

As the Bible was written over the span of 1600 years, it was originally written in three languages: Hebrew, Aramaic, and Koine Greek. These were the common languages of the people at the time and place it was written. Today, the Bible has been translated into over 700 languages and partially translated into over 2,800 additional languages. However, numerous people groups still do not have a translation of the Bible in their native language.

KEY POINTS
- 2 Testaments, Old and New
- 66 books
- Written in 3 languages
- 3 types of translations
- Inspired by God for instruction

When someone creates a Bible translation, they seek to balance the exact translation of the words with the meaning best conveyed in the new language. Thankfully, this work is guided by the Holy Spirit, who instructs us in all things.

When scripture is quoted, you will often see a notation after the verse in parentheses indicating the translation. For example, KJV stands for King James Version, and NIV stands for New International Version.

There are three basic styles of Bible translations - word-for-word translations, thought-for-thought translations, and paraphrase translations. You will find much debate in the Christian community about the "correct" Bible, but we believe God has inspired the Bible's translations, just as He inspired the original writers. Thus, we do not hold to there being a single correct translation. We just want you to find one you will enjoy reading, and READ!

A **word-for-word translation** translates the Bible from the original language word by word. This may make for thoughts we do not understand in our language if the original used a phrase whose direct translation does not convey the intended meaning of the text in the new language. For example, consider the English idiom "It's raining cats and dogs." If we translated that into another language directly, they might wonder why on earth there were animals falling from the sky, and not understand that we mean it to be raining heavily. Examples of word-for-word translations include the New American Standard Bible (NASB) and the King James Version (KJV).

A **thought-for-thought** translation, on the other hand, translates the text in a way that accurately reflects the meaning of the original text. In these translations, "it's raining cats and dogs" might be translated into a phrase in that language that means it is raining heavily." Examples of thought-for-thought translations include the Christian Standard Bible (CSB) and the New International Version (NIV).

Lastly, a **paraphrase translation** rephrases the original text to capture its overall meaning without necessarily preserving word-for-word or thought-for-thought precision. The Message Bible (MSG) is one of the most well-known examples of this type of translation. It's important to note that this kind of translation is often controversial within traditional Christian contexts.

In this study, we have used the English Standard Version (ESV) for most quotations, but have used other translations, based on the ease with which it conveys the meaning of the verse.

ENRICH - *Let's learn more*

Grab your Bible and find out which translation you have. If you have more than one Bible at home, do this for each one. If you use a Bible app, write down the translation(s) you use most. Then, next to each translation, note what type of translation it is.

KJV   *Word-for-word translation*

What types of translations are you drawn to? Which translation is your favorite?

NURTURE - *Let's apply it to our lives*

As of the writing of this edition, there are over 3,658 languages with at least some portion of the Bible translated. However, this still leaves 3% of people without a Bible translation in their native language. You can read more and find out how you might help spread God's Word at Wycliff Global Alliance online.

THANKS - *Let's thank God for this wisdom*

In the box below, write a short prayer thanking God for what He has revealed to you today and asking Him for further insight.

Day 3

TEACH - *Let's learn*

Now that you know more about the Bible and why you should read it often, let's talk about *how* to read your Bible. There are many books and Bible studies on this topic, but we will keep it as simple as we can for this study.

> "He went up on the mountain by Himself to pray; and when it was evening, He was there alone."
> Matt 14:23

Pick a time and location.

Quiet Time - that is what many Christians call the time they have set aside to read their Bible and pray. The reason for this name is that having a time that is quiet and free from distractions, such as young kids, is essential to connecting with our Lord. This might look like getting up earlier than the rest of your household. It might look like having a prayer closet to use, like in the movie *War Room*. Whatever it looks like for you, it needs to be something you can do daily.

When is the best time? The Bible instructs us, "You shall meditate on it day and night, so that you may be careful to do according to all that is written in it" (Joshua 1:8). However, as a new believer or someone new to Bible study, the crucial thing is to establish the habit of spending time with God, regardless of the specific timing. Remember that the primary objective is nurturing your relationship with Jesus. Thus, your aim is to become better acquainted with Him through spending time in His Word.

KEY POINTS
- Pick a time and location.
- Decide what to read.
- Pray before you begin.
- Journal what the Holy Spirit says.

Decide what to read.

Once you know where and when you will spend daily time set apart for God, you should decide what you will study in His Word. Is it going to be a Bible study, or will you choose to read from the Bible on your own? Even if you sometimes (or often) use a pre-written Bible study, I would encourage you to read the Bible alone as well. Let the Holy Spirit speak to your heart.

You don't have to start at the beginning of the Bible and read all the way through, though that is an excellent method. Simply select a book of the Bible that you feel drawn to and start there. Reading through John is often suggested as a good place to begin for those recently saved. We have discovered immense comfort in reading through the Psalms. If you prefer a narrative, the Gospels or the historical books in the Old Testament offer compelling stories. Depending on your life's season and schedule, you can read as much or as little each day as you desire. One common suggestion is to read a chapter a day, but even reading a few verses is better than nothing.

Pray before you begin.

Anytime you begin to study the Bible, you should start in prayer, asking the Holy Spirit to guide you and teach you. He is the one who can open your eyes to the truths He wants to reveal to you. Thus, seek Him in prayer at the beginning and end of each study session. Listen to Him throughout the study session as well.

Journal what the Holy Spirit says.

In the last chapter, we talked about keeping a prayer journal. It is also important to keep a journal of what the Holy Spirit says to you as you read His Word. What new aspects of God did He show you? Note what verses you are reading, any insights from those verses, the date, and anything else that comes to mind as you are studying.

ENRICH - *Let's learn more*

Read Matthew 6:6 and Psalm 1. What do these passages tell us about prayer and Bible study?

NURTURE - *Let's apply it to our lives*

Brainstorm by listing below the various times and locations that would work for you to have Quiet Time with Jesus. We will show you how to refine this list tomorrow.

THANKS - *Let's thank God for this wisdom*

In the box below, write a short prayer thanking God for what He has revealed to you today and asking Him for further insight.

Day 4

TEACH - *Let's learn*

Today, we will focus on how you can make reading scripture a habitual part of your day. The concepts in this section draw inspiration from the bestselling book "Atomic Habits" by James Clear, that teaches you how to form lasting habits.

> "...but his delight
> is in the law of the
> LORD,
> and on His law he
> meditates day
> and night."
> Psalm 1:2

Pick a cue.

The best way to build habits, such as daily Bible reading, is to pick a cue – something that cues you to study your Bible. Such as "Every morning after I make my first cup of coffee, I will open my Bible." The cue needs to be a specific event, not something that is vague. "I will read my Bible every morning" is too vague, as there is no event to trigger the next action. "Morning" could be any time from midnight to 11:59 a.m. The cue needs to be specific so that you will become so used to doing one thing right after the other that you will begin to do it without having to decide to do it consciously.

Stack habits.

One of the best cues you can pick is one that is already a habit. Thus, right after you make your first cup of coffee (already a habit), you begin to read your Bible. This stacking allows you to use the momentum you have already built in creating the first habit to help you build the second habit. If coffee isn't your thing, maybe your cue is after brushing your teeth or returning from your morning jog. The cue is not as important as whether or not it is an established habit.

KEY POINTS
- Pick a cue.
- Stack habits.
- Make reading your Bible easy.
- Make reading your Bible enjoyable.

Make reading your Bible easy

By nature, we are generally lazy creatures, us humans. So, make reading your Bible easy. You should make it easier to do the habit than to avoid it. Thus, put your Bible, a notebook, and pen on the table next to where you will sit down with your coffee each morning so that it is already there and ready. Combining this with your already established practice of drinking coffee in that spot, you will naturally begin to reach for your Bible at that time.

Another way to make your Bible study easy is to make it manageable. If you don't have time to read an entire chapter, just read a few verses. When one author, Carolyn, had a toddler, only 5-minute increments worked for her, as getting up early was just not possible on too little sleep. Candy, on the other hand, is currently retired and able to spend 2 to 3 hours each day reading and studying scripture. The amount of time you have available will change as your seasons of life change.

Make reading your Bible enjoyable.

If something is enjoyable, we repeat it. If you enjoy long, luxurious baths, you find ways to do that often. Enjoy reading, and you will find any excuse to have a book with you. Reading your Bible and spending time with Jesus should be the same way. So, determine what makes it enjoyable for you. Having time alone? Playing praise and worship music? Reading your Bible while enjoying your first cup of coffee? Using fun pens and stickers to make notes? Journaling in a beautiful notebook? Determine what will make it enjoyable and build it into your habit. These things shouldn't be WHY you read your Bible but to help develop the habit.

ENRICH - *Let's learn more*

The word "meditation" often gets a bad reputation in traditional Christian circles, yet it is used 23 times in the Bible, mainly in the book of Psalms. It means to ponder or think about. Spending time reading and praying, as we have described in this chapter, is a form of meditation. Search for verses on meditation in the Bible and note the references here.

NURTURE - *Let's apply it to our lives*

Let's apply what we have learned about habit forming to create our habit cycle. Fill in the diagram below.

What will be your specific CUE?

What habit does this STACK with?

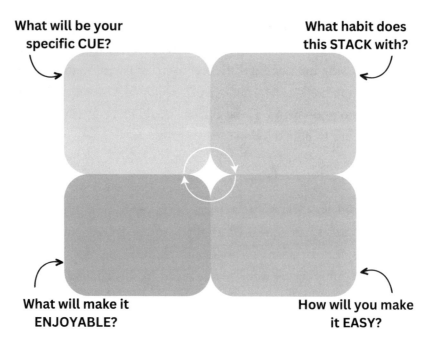

What will make it ENJOYABLE?

How will you make it EASY?

THANKS - *Let's thank God for this wisdom*

In the box below, write a short prayer thanking God for what He has revealed to you today and asking Him for further insight.

Day 5

TEACH - *Let's learn*

Today, let's look at a specific system you can use to take you from Bible *reading* to Bible *study*. It is the process of using the 5 Ws - Who, When, Where, Why, and What.

Step 1 - Who

Who wrote the book? To whom did he write it? Is it stated in the text? If not, some commentaries could tell you or let you know if the author is known. We don't know who wrote every book of the Bible, which is also important to note.

Step 2 - When

When was it written? What events were taking place at the time, both in the historical and biblical contexts? You might have to rely on a good commentary or trustworthy online resource here. Some online resources will be given shortly.

Step 3 - Where

Where was the book written? Is that important? Sometimes, we don't know where an author was when he wrote the book. Other times, it gives rich context to the writing, such the letters Paul wrote to the various churches while he was in prison. Where do the events of the book take place, such as in Egypt, Jerusalem, etc.? How is the location important to the story?

Step 4 - Why

Why did the author write this book? Do they tell you the reason in the text? For example, in Luke 1:1-4, the author, Luke, tells us plainly that he wrote the book to lay out an orderly account of the things that happened in the life of Jesus that we might believe. "Inasmuch as many have undertaken to compile a narrative of the things that have been accomplished among us, just as those who from the beginning were eyewitnesses and ministers of the word have delivered them to us, it seemed good to me also, having followed all things closely for some time past, to write an orderly account for you, most excellent Theophilus, **that you may have certainty concerning the things you have been taught**" (Luke 1:1-4).

KEY POINTS
- *Who* wrote the book? To whom?
- *When* was it written?
- *Where* was it written? Where does it take place?
- *Why* was it written?
- *What* does it tell us about God/Jesus?

Step 5 - What

What does the book say? What are the main themes and biblical principles that are being taught through this book? Most importantly, what does it tell us about God/Jesus? Remember that the Bible was written to teach us about God and to tell us about the promise of salvation through Jesus. Thus, every book of the Bible, even those that do not mention Him, have a thread running through them about how Jesus will come to earth, die, and be resurrected for our sins. Look for that thread in each book you read.

Resources

When studying your Bible, you should always rely first and foremost on the teaching of the Holy Spirit. He will instruct you in all things. Second, use the Bible to define biblical words and concepts. This is where a good concordance is helpful. A concordance is a list of words used in the Bible along with the references where they are used so that you can look up those verses. There are websites, such as bluoletterbible.org or biblegateway.com that you can also use. We have a list of resources in the back of this book, as well.

ENRICH - *Let's learn more*

The style of Bible study that we use at The Ruby Tent is referred to as Inductive Bible Study. Do an online search for Inductive Bible Study, in particular resources by Kay Arthur.

NURTURE - *Let's apply it to our lives*

Let's practice with what you just learned using a very short book as an example. Read the book of Philemon in the New Testament. It is just 25 verses long. Additionally, the book tells you exactly who wrote it, to whom, and why. See if you can identify each of the 5Ws for this short book.

Who

_____
_____
_____
_____
_____
_____

When

_____
_____
_____
_____
_____
_____

Where

_____
_____
_____
_____
_____
_____

Why

_____
_____
_____
_____
_____
_____

What

_____
_____
_____
_____
_____
_____

THANKS - *Let's thank God for this wisdom*

In the box below, write a short prayer thanking God for what He has revealed to you today, and asking Him for further insight.

Want to learn more about how to study the Bible? We dive deeper into studying the Bible - insights into how to do word studies and use biblical resources - in our stand-alone study on How to Study the Bible. This will be part of The Ruby Tent beginning in early 2024. We would love for you to join us!

Come join your sisters at

THE RUBY TENT

And [Jesus] came to Nazareth, where He had been brought up. And *as was His custom,* He went *to the synagogue* on the Sabbath day.

Luke 4:16

Church Home

God created us to live in community with one another. We are not solitary creatures, even if introverts like Carolyn wish that were true. Thus, our relationship with Jesus is not a singular relationship, but it is part of the more significant relationship of Jesus with His bride,- the church.

In this chapter, we will learn:

☑ Why we need to be a member of a church, and

☑ How to choose a church home using four aspects:

      T - Theology
      E - Energy
      N - Nourishment
      T - Testimony

Father, direct each of us to the congregation you have for us, where we can serve and grow as part of the bride of Christ. Amen.

Day 1

TEACH - Let's learn

In the beginning, God created the heavens and the earth. But did you know that He chose you before that?! Ephesians 1:4 says, "He chose us in him before the foundation of the world, that we should be holy and blameless before Him." He knew you - what you would like to eat, who your parents would be, your personality - before He formed the earth! And just like a parent knows a baby is coming and prepares a place for them, He created a special place for you to live and to worship.

> "He chose us in him before the foundation of the world..."
> Ephesians 1:4

As a new believer, finding a cozy and supportive home base is just as important as a baby having a family to nurture and provide for them. You crave a space that fosters growth and comfort. Think about it: God's kiddos aren't meant to wander alone! We are part of a grander community called the Body of Christ. And, just like a body requires all its parts to work together, we need each other to thrive.

In 1 Corinthians 12, Paul describes the Body of Christ and why we need each other. We each have our own talents and needs, and we are meant to work together as a cohesive unit to bring glory to God. You need the encouragement and support of other believers and they need what you have to offer. "God arranged the members in the body, each one of them, as he chose" (1 Corinthians 12:18). Being a part of a church is about fulfilling our role within the Church.

KEY POINTS
- God created us for community.
- He has a unique place in the Body of Christ for each of us.
- God tells us to meet together.
- It was Jesus' regular practice to go to the temple.

God says we need to assemble together. "Not neglecting to meet together, as is the habit of some, but encouraging one another, and all the more as you see the Day drawing near" (Hebrews 10:25). Today, "meetings" are not one of our favorite things. Meetings for work, and meetings for school; most of us do not want to add to the list with church meetings. However, put simply, we should go because God asks us to go. He knows what is best for us. We will be blessed and will bless others in our obedience to attend church.

Further, we need to follow Jesus' example. Luke 4:16 tells us He went to the temple, as was His habit. Just as we discussed building the habit of Bible reading, you should commit to building a church attendance habit and not let things keep you from going. And they will! Satan does not want you to attend church and worship God with other believers. He knows how powerful it will be. Thus, it will seem like everything that can go wrong on Sunday morning does. Go anyway. Even if you are tired, even if you just had a fight with your spouse, even if you yelled at your kids to get them ready. Go anyway. (You may need to repent of your behavior.) But go anyway! Eventually, going will become easier as it becomes a habit. You will look forward to it!

Whenever possible, go to a local church in person. Online church is great for many reasons and seasons, but we do not believe it replaces worshipping with other believers in person. Attending church will give you a chance to meet like-minded believers. You will begin to build a family - older people who can be 'parents/grandparents', and men and women who will become brothers and sisters.

ENRICH - *Let's learn more*

Are you currently a member of a local church? If so, do you know their doctrinal statement? Many churches require you to attend a class where they teach you about their church before you can become a member. That class usually includes information on their doctrine. Look up your church's doctrinal statement online or get a copy from the pastor.

If you do not regularly attend a specific church, find several in your area and compare their doctrinal statements. Does anything stand out to you?

NURTURE - *Let's apply it to our lives*

Is it hard to attend church on Sundays, or do you look forward to it? Without judgment, journal in the space below your thoughts on church attendance. Then, review those thoughts to see if there are things God brings to mind that will encourage your attendance.

THANKS - *Let's thank God for this wisdom*

In the box below, write a short prayer thanking God for what He has revealed to you today and asking Him for further insight.

Day 2

TEACH - *Let's learn*

How do you choose a church home? What should you look for to determine which one to join? You may be currently looking, or you might be happily settled in a church you love, but each of us comes to a point where we might have to decide to find a new church home. A move, job relocation, church split, doctrinal changes from a new pastor, there are many reasons why even those happily settled might find themselves looking again for a church home one day. **The only thing that matters in choosing a church is this - does God want you there?** You'll need to figure out that through prayer. However, while you are praying, we have four tips that can help you search for the right church.

> "But as it is, God arranged the members in the body, each one of them, as he chose."
> 1 Corinthians 12:18

The four things you should consider when looking for your *TENT* are *theology, energy, nourishment,* and *testimony.* We will look at each of these over the next four days.

NOTE: *We do not promote one denomination over another in this study but present general principles that can be applied regardless of your preferences.*

T - Theology

The most important thing to consider in a church is their theology - what they believe. This is why we looked at churches' doctrinal statements yesterday. Specifically, look at what they say about the person and work of Jesus. Jesus' divinity should be the church's primary focus: He was the Son of God who died, was buried, and rose again and now sits at the Father's right hand and intercedes for us.

Next, what do they say about salvation? What is required for salvation? Question any church that teaches that more than the finished work of Jesus on the cross is necessary.

KEY POINTS
- God has a specific church in mind for you.
- Consider a church's theology - who is Jesus, and what is required for salvation?

If you grew up in a church, you may want to continue in that denomination, or you may want to try a church that is not affiliated with an established denomination. The tenents of each denomination are easily found so that you can make an educated decision. For example, Baptists and Methodists are similar, but their beliefs on baptism differ.

Lastly, we couldn't speak about theology without warning about theology changing in specific denominations. The Methodist church is one in which there has been a split, recent to the time of writing this study, over theology. Individual churches in the denomination are deciding what they believe and whether they will stay or switch to another denomination. If you find yourself in a church whose theology seems to have changed from when you joined, take time to pray and study the scriptures. Always use God's Word as a guide to correct theology. If the changes are in keeping with God's Word, then there shouldn't be cause for alarm. However, if the changes are moving away from the Word of God, it is time to pray that God directs you to a new church home.

ENRICH - *Let's learn more*

What does your denomination believe? Do you have a copy of the tenets of the faith? Search online and review them. Note where they describe who Jesus is and what is required for salvation. What aspects are essential to you in finding a denomination?

NURTURE - *Let's apply it to our lives*

Have you been hurt before by a particular denomination or a specific church's beliefs? Take some time to pray through that now. Ask God to show you the lessons and growth you can take from that experience so that you can find the church home God has for you.

THANKS - *Let's thank God for this wisdom*

In the box below, write a short prayer thanking God for what He has revealed to you today and asking Him for further insight.

Day 3

TEACH - *Let's learn*

When finding a church home, you need to look at several aspects of the group of believers before deciding to become a member. The first one is the *theology* of the church. The next one is the E - *Energy* of the church.

E - Energy

Candy and her husband spent a year living full-time in an RV, traveling around the United States. Each Sunday, she would find a church in that area to attend. It was definitely a box of chocolates as she never truly knew what she was going to get!

"O come, let us worship and bow down..."
Psalm 95:6

Attend enough churches, even in the same denomination, as Candy did, and you will see that each church has its own unique energy. Some are loud with lots of movement. Some might be dead, with no one smiling or fully participating in worship. Though we doubt any of us would want to attend a church that is dead, and we certainly wouldn't recommend it, you might prefer something more mellow than the non-stop energy of a church with a live band. Or, maybe the loud band and a lively crowd are the perfect worship experience for you. Our point is that until you actually attend a church for yourself, you will not know what the energy and presence feel like.

The style of preaching is also something to be considered. Some preachers use lots of stories about themselves to illustrate points. Some preach topical series like "Marriage God's Way" and use passages throughout the Bible. Some preach straight through a particular book. Some preachers use Greek and Hebrew word studies in their sermons. The two consulting pastors for The Ruby Tent have very different preaching styles, yet we enjoy and respect both immensely. Find one you believe God is using to speak to you, but check that his doctrine aligns with scripture.

KEY POINTS
- The church's energy is an essential aspect of whether you will feel at home there.
- Listen to the pastor and ensure his doctrine lines up with scripture, regardless of his preaching style.

You may like the pastor but may not enjoy his delivery. Some pastors seem angry. Some are more like storytelling grandfathers. Then, there are the "hoppers," those who jump around and pace on stage. If you are distracted by the delivery of the sermon, you will have trouble focusing on the content of the message. Thus, find a pastor whose delivery style adds to the message for you. The style we enjoy will be different for each of us, which adds to the flavor of the body of Christ!

Regardless of the energy of the church, remember that theology overrides energy. If the theology is not sound, your connecting with the church's energy does not matter.

ENRICH - *Let's learn more*

Different denominations also have very different energies - and different is good! We just need to take that into account. Episcopalians are more formal in their worship. Baptists are typically more subdued. Non-denominational churches vary but often are more energetic. How would you describe the energy of your denomination? Does it match the energy that you enjoy? Is your church typical of the energy in your denomination?

NURTURE - *Let's apply it to our lives*

If you are currently a member of a church, describe your pastor's preaching style below. What elements of his style add to the worship experience for you? If you do not currently have a church home, based on what we have described, what would you look for in a pastor?

THANKS - *Let's thank God for this wisdom*

In the box below, write a short prayer thanking God for what He has revealed to you today and asking Him for further insight.

Day 4

TEACH - *Let's learn*

We have looked at a church's *theology* and its *energy*. Now, let's look at the next aspect: its ability to nourish you. The next letter is *N - Nourishment*.

N - Nourishment

A baby needs the proper nourishment to grow. As a new believer, you need the proper nourishment as well, or you will not grow as vital spiritually as you could. Being a part of a body of believers is one way we get nourishment. But each church provides different programs and services, which will nourish us in different ways.

"...worship him
who made
heaven and earth,
the sea and the
springs of water."
Rev 14:7

Nourishment is about how you fit into the church. Are there people or programs that meet your individual needs and the needs of your family? Large churches usually have more to offer for different groups, such as a kids ministry, a youth group for teenagers, or maybe a singles ministry for young adults, women's ministries, men's ministries, and outreach. However, don't dismiss the possibility of a smaller church. These churches can seem more like a family where everyone works and worships together regardless of age.

We both have been members of large churches with programs of every type, as well as members of smaller congregations. Carolyn and her family currently are members of a church with less than 50 on the roll and have grown there more than in any previous church. She and her husband prayed and followed God's leading, even when He led them to a church very different from the one in their last town. And that is our prayer for you, that you will follow God's lead in choosing any church home.

KEY POINTS
- Churches offer different programs and opportunities.
- You need a church where you will grow in your faith, regardless of its size.
- Pour into your church as they pour into you.

You can't pour from an empty cup. Thus, you need to find a church pouring into you and filling your cup. But notice that the saying is you can't POUR from an empty cup. The implication here is that you are pouring! You should be pouring into your church just as they pour into you. God makes our cups overflow. Thus, we have enough to pour into others, and yet still be full ourselves! Thus, we should be serving in our church. God has gifted each member of the Body gifts intended to be used for the church. Make sure you are using your gifts, whether that gift is to teach, pray, or clean the bathrooms!

When feeding a baby, we may believe breastfeeding is ideal. Yet, if that is not possible, we feed the baby as best we can with high-quality formula because 'fed' is genuinely best, regardless of how that is accomplished. Similarly, it may be wonderful to have multitudes of different programs and opportunities to serve, but if those are not helping you grow, find a church where you will grow, regardless of its program offerings. And then, SERVE!

ENRICH - *Let's learn more*

Read 1 Corinthians 12: 4-11. Here, Paul describes the gifts of the Spirit. We believe this is a partial list. There are other lists, even in the Bible, that name other gifts. You can use this list as a reference. What are your gifts? In what ways has God called you to serve the church? Our gift is teaching, whether in math, public speaking, or God's Word. If you don't know your gifts, pray that God will reveal them to you. He loves to show us the gifts He has given us.

NURTURE - *Let's apply it to our lives*

What programs does your church offer, or what programs would you look for in a church? What are your current needs, such as a nursery or a singles ministry? Are there programs your church offers that you would be a good fit for, yet you aren't involved with? Why or why not? Pray that God will help you participate fully in the life of your church.

THANKS - *Let's thank God for this wisdom*

In the box below, write a short prayer thanking God for what He has revealed to you today and asking Him for further insight.

Day 5

TEACH - *Let's learn*

We have looked at the first three aspects of finding a church home - a church's *theology*, its *energy*, and its ability to *nourish* and be nourished by you. Today, we will look at the last aspect in finding a church home, its *T - Testimony*.

> "And [Jesus] asked them, 'But who do you say that I am?'"
> Mark 8:29

T - Testimony

According to the Merriam-Webster dictionary, a testimony is "a public profession of religious experience." Thus, when someone tells you how God has moved in their life, that is a testimony. So, when searching for a church home, you should find out what each church says about itself. When and why was it founded? Why does it exist today? What does it say it believes? (We covered that last one on day 2 of this chapter.) It may be fun, challenging, and rewarding to be in on the beginning of a new church, but check to see why they are new. Or, maybe it is an older church, but it has not been growing or changing in years. These would be important to know before deciding to become a member.

What is the main emphasis of the church? For example, is it a mission-oriented church that sends out missionaries and mission teams regularly? Or, perhaps, it is focused on evangelism and strives to reach people who have not heard the gospel. It might be a church that prays, or one that faithfully serves its community. What are they known for? Does its emphasis match what God has called you to do with your gifts?

God's guidance here is of utmost importance because, even within major denominations, churches have different purposes and goals based on why they were established and the strengths and weaknesses of their members.

KEY POINTS
- What does the church say about itself?
- What is its main emphasis?
- Does that emphasis match your gifts, so that you fit as a member of that body of believers?

Many churches have a membership class that they encourage (or perhaps require) prospective new members to take before joining the church. We believe this is very valuable, as it gives you time to learn about the church's testimony, which is often the main focus of the class. If your church does not offer this type of class, ask to sit down for coffee with the pastor or a church elder who can answer these questions for you.

We cannot close this chapter without a reminder that the very first and most important thing is - does God want you there? Is the

Holy Spirit calling you to this church? You will not be able to discern this without prayer. If He calls you to a particular church, nothing we said in this chapter is very important. If He isn't calling you to that church, let nothing we wrote convince you otherwise. We hope that these aspects of choosing a church will help guide your attendance as you pray for discernment in where God is calling you to grow and serve. Until you know what God wants for you, continue to attend church, but do not formally join any church as a member.

ENRICH - *Let's learn more*

Read the account of the formation of the first church in Acts 2:40-47. What stands out to you about this church that is different than churches today? How could we, as believers, love each other more like those in the first church?

NURTURE - *Let's apply it to our lives*

If you are a member of a church currently, why did you become a member? What is your testimony of that experience?

If you are not a member of a church, what is your testimony of how Jesus became Lord of your life? Write it out below!

THANKS - *Let's thank God for this wisdom*

In the box below, write a short prayer thanking God for what He has revealed to you today and asking Him for further insight.

Whoever walks with the *wise* becomes wise, *but* the companion of fools will suffer harm.

Proverbs 13:20

Companions

Look at a person's friends, and you will be able to tell much about them. Are their friends loud and obnoxious? Are they studious and kind? You know the old saying, "Birds of a feather flock together." Old sayings don't become old sayings without having some truth to them.

In this chapter, we will learn:

- ☑ Why we need friends,

- ☑ What types of friends we need,

- ☑ How to find a mentor,

- ☑ How to find your sisters, and

- ☑ How to pour into other believers.

Father, bring us mentors to guide us, friends to walk alongside us, and mentees on whom we can pour out your love and truth. Amen.

Day 1

TEACH - *Let's learn*

Why do we need friends? If you are an extrovert, like Candy, you probably think you need friends as much as you need air to breathe, and this question is ridiculous. If you are an introvert, like Carolyn, you have actually asked yourself this question, in all seriousness, at least once in your life. But regardless of whether or not you are an introvert, we do need friends. As we have said before, God designed us for community. We cannot have community without relationships with other people.

> "A friend loves at all times, and a brother is born for adversity."
> Proverbs 17:17

Why did God create us to live in community? Because He created us to love Him and bring Him glory. Thus, we were created for a relationship. When God created Adam, He said, "It is not good that the man should be alone; I will make him a helper fit for him" (Genesis 2:18). Thus, God states in the second chapter of the Bible that we were created for relationship with other humans as well. Science has shown that our brains are actually wired for social connection, which makes sense if God literally made us for it.

If we were created for community, then we should operate best when living in a healthy community. Science has shown that this is true. "A review of 38 studies found that adult friendships, especially high-quality ones that provide social support and companionship, significantly predict well-being and can protect against mental health issues such as depression and anxiety—and those benefits persist across the life span" (Abrams, 2023).

KEY POINTS
- God created us to live in community.
- Our community should consist of other believers.
- In our walk with Jesus, we need three types of friends: those pouring into us, those walking with us, and those we are pouring into.

The quote by Jim Rohn, "You are the average of the five people you spend the most time with" is backed up by scripture. Proverbs 13:20 says, "whoever walks with the wise becomes wise, but the companion of fools will suffer harm." If you are addicted to drugs, one of the first things a counselor will tell you is that you have to change who you hang around. This is because those you hang around usually give you the drugs, use them with you, or enable you to use them. When you become a new believer in Christ, you might also have to change who you hang around. At the least, you will need to add to your circle of friends people who can help you grow in your walk with Jesus.

In our walk with Jesus, we need three types of friends: those pouring into us, those walking with us, and those we are pouring into. We will look at that more tomorrow.

ENRICH - *Let's learn more*

Read Proverbs 13:20 and 17:9. What do these verses tell us about finding true friendship?

Read Proverbs 22:24-25 and 17:9. What do these verses tell us will hurt true friendship?

NURTURE - *Let's apply it to our lives*

Spend some time today praying about your circle of friends. Who in your circle does God want you to keep close? Who does God want you to add to your circle? Is there anyone you know of that God is leading you to remove from your circle? Removing friends is painful, but if God leads you, He will help you walk through that process. We will talk more about that in this chapter.

THANKS - *Let's thank God for this wisdom*

In the box below, write a short prayer thanking God for what He has revealed to you today and asking Him for further insight.

Day 2

TEACH - *Let's learn*

Yesterday, we looked at why it is so important to have friends. Today, we will look at what types of friends you need.

In our walk with Jesus, we need three types of friends: those pouring into us (mentors), those walking with us (sisters), and those we are pouring into (mentees). We see this example throughout scripture, but one clear example is Moses and his relationships.

> "Faithful are the wounds of a friend, But deceitful are the kisses of an enemy."
> Prov 27:6 (NASB)

In Exodus 18:13-27, Jethro sees Moses trying to do too much and councils him on a better way to handle so many people's disputes. Jethro, Moses' father-in-law, is a mentor to Moses, advising him on a course of action that helped in his difficulty. Note that Moses recognized that there was a difficulty but did not realize that there was a better way. His father-in-law saw the better way since he was older and wiser. That is what we need in a mentor – someone who has walked the path before us and has gained insight from it.

Moses also had people walking alongside him. In Exodus 4:10-17, when Moses told God he was not good at speaking, God sent Aaron to go with Moses and speak for him. Aaron was Moses' brother, born to the same Israelite parents in Egypt before God delivered the Israelites from slavery.

KEY POINTS
There are three types of relationships that we need when we are growing in our faith:
- mentors,
- sisters, and
- mentees.

Aaron wasn't the only family member who walked alongside Moses as he obeyed God in delivering the Israelites from Egypt. Moses' sister, Miriam, was with Moses as well. In Micah 6:4, God is reminding the people of Israel of all He had done for them, and He includes Miriam in the list of those who helped bring them out of Egypt. "For I brought you up from the land of Egypt and redeemed you from the house of slavery, and I sent before you Moses, Aaron, and Miriam."

As we learn and grow in our faith, we need to be serving others just as we have been served. Jesus said, "If anyone would be first, he must be last of all and servant of all" (Mark 9:35). Moses taught Joshua what he had learned, and when the time came, God appointed Joshua to lead the Israelites after Moses' death (Deuteronomy 31:14).

Thus, Moses had a mentor (Jethro), someone who walked with him (Aaron), and a mentee (Joshua). Similarly, having a 'Jethro', an 'Aaron', and a 'Joshua' in our own lives will help us grow in our faith.

Your **sisters** walk along side you.

Your **mentor** pours into you.

Your **mentee** is someone you pour into.

ENRICH - *Let's learn more*

Just as we have always looked to see what Jesus did in prayer, reading scripture, and attending church, He, too, had friends and those He was teaching. He also had someone He followed (Hint: Read John 5:19). Identify some of these people in Jesus' life.

NURTURE - *Let's apply it to our lives*

As you begin to try to identify these people in your own life, what concerns do you have? What feelings come up? Journal about this below.

THANKS - *Let's thank God for this wisdom*

In the box below, write a short prayer thanking God for what He has revealed to you today and asking Him for further insight.

Day 3

TEACH - Let's learn

Let's look at the first of these relationships - your mentor.

Mentors pour into us and help us grow. They are willing to look at the situations we find ourselves in with fresh eyes and advise us. We might not even recognize that we need advice, but we allow them into our world and let them look around. We invite their advice when they see we need it. We have given them permission to speak into our circumstances when they see necessary.

> "Oil and perfume make the heart glad, and the sweetness of a friend comes from his earnest counsel."
> Prov 27:9

Mentors can be similar to spiritual parents. In 1 Timothy 1:2, Paul indicates that he is Timothy's spiritual father and mentor. "To Timothy, my true child in the faith: Grace, mercy, and peace from God the Father and Christ Jesus our Lord." Parents guide and teach their children; spiritual parents guide and teach someone to learn and grow in their faith. This person is not necessarily the person who introduced you to Jesus or taught you about salvation, but it could be.

You may not have a spiritual parent, but you can find a spiritual mentor. If someone told you about Jesus or walked you through the steps of salvation, they may be a good choice for a mentor. If your church has a mentor program that matches people together, take advantage of it. And if none of these exist for you, the best choice would be to join a women's Bible study or participate in a women's ministry and get to know the ladies involved. Pray that God will lead you to someone who can be that mentor in your life.

KEY POINTS
- A mentor can be a type of spiritual parent.
- You find mentors by getting involved in your church or local Christian activities.
- Look for someone who exhibits the fruit of the Spirit.

Remember that this is a relationship, first and foremost. It can be very awkward to approach someone and ask them to be your mentor. Instead, we suggest you find someone you would like to mentor you and ask them to coffee. Spend time building a relationship with them. If they are more mature in their faith, this relationship you are building might naturally develop into a mentoring type of relationship. You might also get to know them well enough that asking them to be a mentor to you might not feel awkward anymore.

A good mentor will be more mature in their faith. Their behavior should demonstrate the fruit of the Spirit: "love, joy, peace, patience, kindness, goodness, faithfulness, gentleness, self-control" (Galatians 5:22-23). You should see evidence in their life of good decisions and giving good advice that is in keeping with scripture. Paul describes his mentoring relationship with Timothy as follows, "You, however, have followed my teaching, my conduct, my aim in life, my faith, my patience, my love, my steadfastness" (2 Timothy 3:10). Note how the list of things that Paul describes Timothy experienced matches closely the fruit of the Spirit.

ENRICH - *Let's learn more*

Naomi and Ruth also had a mentor/mentee relationship. Read Ruth 2:18 - 3:5. What aspects of mentoring do you see described in the story?

NURTURE - *Let's apply it to our lives*

As you begin to try to identify these people in your life, what concerns do you have? What feelings come up? Journal about this below.

THANKS - *Let's thank God for this wisdom*

In the box below, write a short prayer thanking God for what He has revealed to you today and asking Him for further insight.

Day 4

TEACH - *Let's learn*

Mentors pour into us, but as we grow, we must begin pouring into others. We need to become the mentor! Someone we mentor is called a mentee.

Just as some are further down the path than we are, others are not as far along. While we have trusted Jesus as our Lord, there are those in our lives who have not. We can talk to them and share the good news of Jesus with them. Thus, we can begin pouring into others from the very start of our walk. If you need help sharing the gospel, you can use the page "How do I become saved?" in the Introduction of this book.

> "Many Samaritans
> from that town believed in
> him because of the
> woman's
> testimony, 'He told me all
> that I ever did.'"
> John 4:39

After we begin to mature in our faith, there are new Christians whom we can mentor and guide in their first steps. God will bring those people into your life, pray for the opportunity, and watch what happens. You can also volunteer to serve in the nursery or children's ministry. Children need adults who will love them and demonstrate the love of Christ. Serving your church in this way will bless you, and you will bless others.

When we have walked with Jesus for many seasons and through many trials, we can become what some of us southern Christian women call a 'Titus 2 woman,' from the description in that chapter of the Bible. "Older women likewise are to be reverent in behavior, not slanderers or slaves to much wine. They are to teach what is good, and so train the young women to love their husbands and children, to be self-controlled, pure, working at home, kind, and submissive to their own husbands, that the word of God may not be reviled" (Titus 2:3-5). As you see from this verse, there is much that an older (read 'more mature') woman can share with those who are younger (both in age and to the faith).

KEY POINTS
- You can, and should, share the gospel with others as soon as you are saved.
- As you grow in your faith, serve in the church and pour into those God brings you.
- As you mature, you will be able to pour into more people and teach more things.

We do not believe this list is exhaustive of what a woman can teach younger women. Paul is giving examples here of things that *can* and *should* be taught. When listing examples, the author might list all that comes to mind, but certainly, it is only intended to be an exhaustive list if the author states as much.

As we have mentioned before, the best place to mentor others is in your local church. By becoming involved in the various ministries that your church offers, you can serve others and share your gifts. Through serving, you will naturally meet others with whom you will build closer bonds and can help them grow.

But do not negate God's ability to bring people into your life from any area or avenue. Live your life reflective of Jesus, and watch what happens. Carolyn shares her story of redemption often with anyone who will listen. One day, after praying for someone to pour into, she received a phone call from a friend at work saying that she had someone she wanted Carolyn to talk to and mentor. What an answer to prayer! God loves to answer those prayers, and He will also bring people into your life at the right time.

ENRICH - *Let's learn more*

Reread Titus 2:3-5 and Galatians 5:22-23. List below the character traits you will need to develop as you grow into someone mature in the faith. (The good news is that it is God who works in you to develop this character, so you don't have to stress!)

NURTURE - *Let's apply it to our lives*

It might be scary to think about needing to mentor someone else, especially if you are new to your walk with Jesus. But as we have said, it is God that does this work through you. He also can handle our fears and remove them. Take some time to talk to Him about how you feel about mentoring others.

THANKS - *Let's thank God for this wisdom*

In the box below, write a short prayer thanking God for what He has revealed to you today and asking Him for further insight.

Day 5

TEACH - Let's learn

Over the last four days, we have considered why we need friends, what types of friends we need, and the unique friendship of a mentor and mentee. Today, let's talk about your friends that walk with you. Your squad!

> "Do not be unequally yoked with unbelievers. For what partnership has righteousness with lawlessness? Or what fellowship has light with darkness?"
> 2 Cor 6:14

Your first question as a new believer might be, "Do all my friends have to be Christians now?" And the answer is No! You don't have to start distancing yourself from your current friends who are not Christians *unless* God tells you to or they negatively affect your relationship with Jesus. You *should*, however, begin telling them about your new relationship with Jesus and praying that they will also be saved. It will be best for your walk with Christ if your closest friends are on the same journey that you are on now. You might even begin finding it easier, or more preferable, to hang out with other Christians as God removes your desire to participate in the sins you once enjoyed. But never fear, for God has the best in mind for you, and if He begins to remove people from your life, it is for your good and His glory.

Some new believers might have few people in their circle who are Christians. So, how do you find other women who are Christians if you do not know any? We have said this many times, but the best way is to find a church home and begin to serve. You should meet many women eager to get to know you better in your home church. Join a women's Bible study and talk to those who attend. Look to see if your church has a women's ministry. A women's ministry is an outreach program in many churches that allows women to meet and encourage one another. If your church offers this type of ministry, we encourage you to participate and see if you can meet other women who can be your mentors, friends, or mentees.

KEY POINTS
- You will need Christian friends.
- You may have to change your friends, but you might not.
- Share the gospel with your friends.
- Join programs at your church to meet people.

Remember that there is only one true church – *one* Body of Christ. Just because there may be more churches in your town than there are streets (if you live in the southern United States, as we do) does not mean we are all separate churches. We are one church, organized into many groups. Thus, check social media for other opportunities for Christian fellowship in your area. There might be women's conferences in your area or events at other churches you can attend. Most church events are not limited to only members of that church, so feel free to attend events at other local churches that you find interesting. The women there would love to meet their sisters from other groups of believers. Don't rule out the possibility that your new Christian bestie might attend a different church than you do.

Lastly, as we hope you know deeply now, talking to God about your friendships, concerns, hurts, and desires is what He wants you to do more than anything. Go to Him continuously as you navigate your friendships.

ENRICH - *Let's learn more*

Spend some time today researching the programs in your church where you might meet friends. Or, go online and see what women's conferences might be coming to your area.

NURTURE - *Let's apply it to our lives*

We have so enjoyed walking through this study with you. We have prayed over you and your walk with Jesus, even though we may not know your name. We would love to be two of those people pouring into you. Connect with us @therubytent on social media or at www.therubytent.com.

We also have a community of believers taking the same courses you are in that we encourage you to join. You might even find your people waiting for you there!

Come join your sisters at

THANKS - *Let's thank God for this wisdom*

In the box below, write a short prayer thanking God for what He has revealed to you today and asking Him for further insight.

Resources and References

Abrams, Z. (2023). *The science of why friendships keep us healthy.* Monitor on Psychology, 54(4), 42. https://www.apa.org/monitor/2023/06/cover-story-science-friendship

Arthur, K., Arthur, D., & De Lacy, P. (2014). *How to study your Bible.* Harvest House Publishers.

BibleGateway.com: A searchable online Bible in over 150 versions and 50 languages. (n.d.). https://biblegateway.com/

Blue Letter Bible. (n.d.). Blue Letter Bible. https://blueletterbible.org/

Clear, J. (2018). *Atomic habits: tiny changes, remarkable results : an easy & proven way to build good habits & break bad ones.* New York, New York, Avery, an imprint of Penguin Random House.

Kendrick, A. (2015). *War Room.* Sony Pictures Releasing.

MacArthur, J. (2013). *Strange fire: The danger of offending the Holy Spirit with counterfeit worship.* Nelson Books.

Merriam-Webster. (n.d.). *Testimony.* In Merriam-Webster.com dictionary. Retrieved October 19, 2023 from https://www.merriam-webster.com/dictionary/testimony

The Bible - Search and Read the Bible Online with Study Tools. (n.d.). biblestudytools.com. https://biblestudytools.com/

Wycliffe Bible Translators. (n.d.). https://wycliffe.org/

Acknowledgements

When you undertake something like writing this book, there are many people to thank. We would like to thank our husbands, Mel Cowan and Bryan Wiley, who put up with our writing in the middle of the night. Thanks to Candy's son and Carolyn's brother, John Warren, for his support. This would NOT have happened without him. Thank you to Carolyn's kids, who put up with her sometimes writing instead of playing. Thank you to Evie, who would help us out any chance we would let her, including photo shoots. Thanks to Adrienne for all her advice on social media and all things tech-related. Thank you to our pastors, Douglas Bell and Chris Twilley, for your support, encouragement, and advice.